Telling Time

by David A. Adler

illustrated by Edward Miller

 HOLIDAY HOUSE · NEW YORK

For Susan and Avery —D. A. A.

To my mom —E. M.

Text copyright © 2019 by David A. Adler
Illustrations copyright © 2019 by Edward Miller
All Rights Reserved
HOLIDAY HOUSE is registered in the U.S. Patent and Trademark Office.
Printed and bound in August 2019 at Toppan Leefung, DongGuan City, China.
www.holidayhouse.com
First Edition
1 3 5 7 9 10 8 6 4 2
Library of Congress Cataloging-in-Publication Data

Names: Adler, David A., author. | Miller, Edward, 1964– illustrator.
Title: Telling time / by David A. Adler ; illustrated by Edward Miller.
Description: First edition. | New York : Holiday House, [2019]
Audience: Ages 6–9. | Audience: K to grade 3.
Identifiers: LCCN 2018015219 | ISBN 978-0-8234-4092-4 (hardcover)
Subjects: LCSH: Time—Juvenile literature. | Time measurements—Juvenile
literature. | Clocks and watches—Juvenile literature.
Classification: LCC QB209.5 .A3495 2019 | DDC 529/.7—dc23 LC record
available at https://lccn.loc.gov/2018015219

ISBN: 978-0-8234-4092-4

Visit www.davidaadler.com for more information on the author, for a list of his books, and to
download teacher's guides and educational materials. You can also learn more about the writing
process, take fun quizzes, and read selected pages from David A. Adler's books.

What time is it?

People ask that a lot. That's because our day goes according to a schedule. There's a time to wake up and a time to go to school. There's a time for breakfast and a time for lunch.

To know the time, you need to be able to read a clock. You need to be able to "tell time."

You also need to know how each **day** is divided into **hours, minutes,** and **seconds.**

A **second** is a relatively short period of time.

10, 9, 8, 7, 6, 5, 4, 3, 2, 1,
Liftoff!

Beyond hours, minutes, and seconds, for most people in the United States and Canada each day is divided into halves, **A.M.** and **P.M.** Each half is twelve hours.

The 12 hours from **midnight** until **noon** are the A.M. hours.

The 12 hours from **noon** until **midnight** are the P.M. hours.

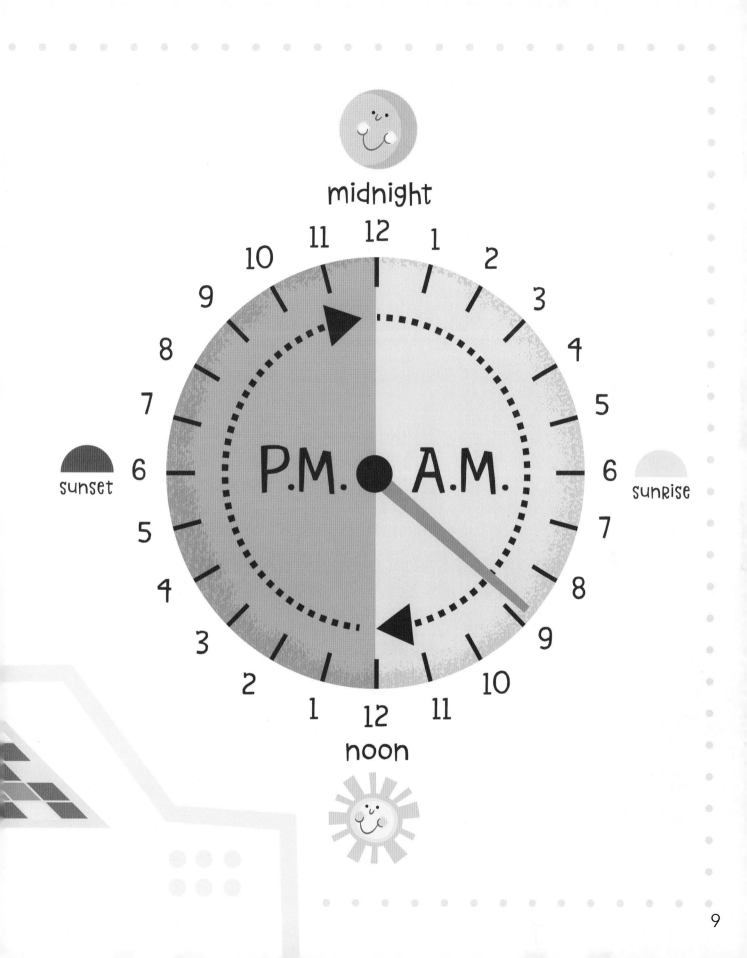

midnight

11 12 1
10 2
9 3
8 4
7 5
sunset 6 P.M. A.M. 6 sunrise
5 7
4 8
3 9
2 10
1 12 11

noon

4:12

hour   minutes

There are two types of clocks, digital and analog. On a **digital clock** there are two sets of numbers separated by two dots, one dot on top of the other. The number to the left of the dots tells us the hour. The number to the right tells us the minutes.

The time on this digital clock is 4:12. This is 12 minutes past 4 o'clock.

This is an **analog clock**. There are twelve numbers and three moving pointers on this clock. The moving pointers are called "**hands**."

With your finger, follow the numbers around the clock. Begin with 12 and move your finger to the 1 and then to the 2. Follow the numbers all the way around until you come back to 12. Your finger moved around the clock in a **"clockwise"** direction. That's the same direction the hands on a clock travel.

The shortest hand on an analog clock is the **hour hand**. It takes the hour hand twelve hours to travel around the clock.

The longer hand is the **minute hand**. It takes one hour (sixty minutes) to travel around the clock.

The thin red hand moves quickly. It's the **second hand**. It takes just sixty seconds (one minute) to travel around the clock.

With an analog clock, when you want to know the time you first look at the hour hand.

Look at this analog clock. The shortest hand, the hour hand, is pointing directly to the 4. The minute hand is pointing to the 12. It's 4 o'clock.

Over the next hour, the hour hand will move from pointing directly to the 4 to pointing directly to the 5. Until it gets there, the time is sometime between 4 o'clock and 5 o'clock.

WATCH YOUR STEP

The time is 4 o'clock plus some minutes.

How many minutes past 4 is it?

To know that, you must check the longer hand, the minute hand.

There are 60 minutes in an hour. There are 12 number-stops on a clock. When you divide 60 by 12 you get 5. It takes the minute hand 5 minutes to travel from one number-stop to the next.

Look at the clock. The minute hand is pointing to the 1. It took the minute hand 5 minutes to travel from the 12 to the 1. The time is 4:05 P.M., 5 minutes past 4.

Now look at the hour hand. It's no longer pointing directly to the 4. It has moved slightly toward the 5. It will take a full hour for the hour hand to move from pointing to the 4 to pointing to the 5.

$$\frac{60}{\div 12}{5}$$

Many analog clocks have four dots or four small lines between adjacent numbers.

For the minute hand, each dot or line represents 1 minute.

Look again at the analog clock. Some time has passed. The minute hand is no longer pointing to the 1. It's pointing to the 3.

What time is it?

The hour hand is between the 4 and the 5. That tells us it's after 4 o'clock but not yet 5 o'clock. The minute hand is pointing to the 3. It takes the minute hand 5 minutes to travel from one number-stop to the next.

The 3 is the third number-stop past the 12.

$$\begin{array}{r} 5 \\ \times\ 3 \\ \hline 15 \end{array}$$

The time is 4:15 P.M., 15 minutes past 4.

More time has passed.

The hour hand is still between the 4 and the 5, but now it's closer to the 5. That tells us it's almost 5 o'clock. The minute hand is pointing to the 10. It takes the minute hand 5 minutes to travel from one number-stop to the next. The 10 is the tenth number-stop past the 12.

An hour is 60 minutes. That means that a half hour is 30 minutes. At 4:30 some people will say the time is "half past four."

Because an hour is 60 minutes, that means a quarter of an hour is 15 minutes. At 4:15 some people will say the time is "a quarter past four."

At 4:45 some people will say the time is "a quarter to five" or "a quarter before five." That's because in 15 more minutes, in a quarter of an hour, it will be 5:00.

MINUTE

SECOND

HOUR

12 1 2 3 4 5 6 7 8 9 10 11

Time flies!

Once you know how to tell time, you can know how long it takes to do things.

If this is the time you began to eat dinner . . .

and this is the time you were done, how long did it take you to eat dinner?

If this is the time you fell asleep last night (on the clock below), and this is the time you woke (on the clock on the next page), how long did you sleep?

Remember, you fell asleep in the P.M. half of the day and woke up in the A.M. half of the day.

Good night!

To know how long you slept, you would have to know how long it was from the time you fell asleep until midnight, 12:00 A.M. That's 3 hours and 30 minutes, or 3½ hours, from 8:30.

You would then add the amount of time from midnight until when you woke up. That's 6 hours.

$$3½$$
$$+6$$
$$=9½$$

Good morning!

I slept 9½ hours.

And now we're ready for a day full of lots of fun
seconds, minutes, and **hours.**

Glossary

A.M. (also a.m. and AM)—The 24-hour day is divided into two periods, each twelve hours. The hours from midnight until noon are the A.M. hours.

Clockwise—The direction the hands on an analog clock move as time passes.

Day—A unit in measuring time. Each day is 24 hours long.

Hour—A unit used in measuring time. Each hour is made up of 60 minutes, which is 3,600 seconds.

Midnight—The very beginning of the A.M. half of the day. It comes in the middle of the night and is written as 12:00 A.M.

Minute—A unit used in measuring time. Each minute is made up of 60 seconds.

Noon—The very beginning of the P.M. half of the day. It comes in the middle of the daylight hours and is written as 12:00 P.M.

P.M. (also p.m. and PM)—The 24-hour day is divided into two periods, each twelve hours. The hours from noon until midnight are the P.M. hours.

Second—A unit used in measuring time. 60 seconds equal one minute.

Author's Note

Sundial
An early type of clock that uses shadows cast by the sun to give the local time. Of course, a sundial is of no use at night after the sun has set.

Daylight Savings Time
A change in clock settings in some places during the summer months that shortens the apparent time of sunlight in the early morning when most people are sleeping and extends it in the evening when most people are awake. Daylight Savings Time is observed in almost the entire United States.

Military Time
Soldiers in the United States Army use what is sometime called military time. They use twenty-four-hour clocks, so there is no A.M. or P.M. 6:00 P.M. would be 18:00 in military time. Twenty-four-hour clocks are also used in many parts of the world, especially for railroad and airline schedules.

Time Zones
The world has been divided from the North Pole to the South Pole into twenty-four times zones. The time is the same within each time zone. The time in the zone just to the east is one hour later. The time in the zone just to the west is one hour earlier. Within times zones, noon marks the time when the sun is approximately directly overhead.